IT'S TIME TO EAT ALMOND PEANUT BUTTER SQUARES

It's Time to Eat ALMOND PEANUT BUTTER SQUARES

Walter the Educator

Silent King Books
A WhichHead Entertainment Imprint

Copyright © 2024 by Walter the Educator

All rights reserved. No part of this book may be reproduced in any manner whatsoever without written per- mission except in the case of brief quotations embodied in critical articles and reviews.

First Printing, 2024

Disclaimer

This book is a literary work; the story is not about specific persons, locations, situations, and/or circumstances unless mentioned in a historical context. Any resemblance to real persons, locations, situations, and/or circumstances is coincidental. This book is for entertainment and informational purposes only. The author and publisher offer this information without warranties expressed or implied. No matter the grounds, neither the author nor the publisher will be accountable for any losses, injuries, or other damages caused by the reader's use of this book. The use of this book acknowledges an understanding and acceptance of this disclaimer.

It's Time to Eat ALMOND PEANUT BUTTER SQUARES is a collectible early learning book by Walter the Educator suitable for all ages belonging to Walter the Educator's Time to Eat Book Series. Collect more books at WaltertheEducator.com

USE THE EXTRA SPACE TO TAKE NOTES AND DOCUMENT YOUR MEMORIES

ALMOND PEANUT BUTTER SQUARES

It's almond peanut butter squares time, hooray!

It's Time to Eat Almond Peanut Butter Squares

A nutty treat for snacktime today!

Creamy and crunchy, sweet and neat,

These squares are the yummiest treat!

With almonds and peanuts, smooth and round,

In every bite, joy is found!

A little chewy, a little sweet,

Almond peanut butter squares can't be beat!

Chomp, chomp, munch! It's fun to chew,

With every bite, there's something new.

Packed with nuts and tasty flair,

Almond peanut butter squares are rare!

Sticky and gooey, held just right,

They give us strength with every bite.

From lunchbox treats to snacktime fun,

These nutty squares are number one!

It's Time to Eat Almond Peanut Butter Squares

Rolled in oats or sprinkled with seeds,

They have all the good stuff our body needs.

With honey or chocolate, or maybe plain,

Almond peanut butter squares are the main!

Soft inside, a crunchy top,

One bite and it's hard to stop!

Healthy, hearty, good and fair,

They're a snack beyond compare!

Full of protein, nutty and sweet,

They're the perfect snack we love to eat!

Perfect for picnics, or after school,

These little squares are super cool!

Made with love and a bit of cheer,

They're the best treat far and near.

Nutty squares, both big and small,

It's Time to Eat

Almond Peanut Butter Squares

Almond peanut butter squares have it all!

So let's all cheer, let's all say,

"Almond peanut butter squares today!"

Creamy, crunchy, healthy, and sweet,

They're the perfect snacktime treat!

Grab a square, let's take a bite,

Nutty squares that feel just right!

Almond peanut butter, soft and fine,

It's Time to Eat
Almond Peanut Butter Squares

The best treat ever, it's square snack time!

ABOUT THE CREATOR

Walter the Educator is one of the pseudonyms for Walter Anderson. Formally educated in Chemistry, Business, and Education, he is an educator, an author, a diverse entrepreneur, and he is the son of a disabled war veteran. "Walter the Educator" shares his time between educating and creating. He holds interests and owns several creative projects that entertain, enlighten, enhance, and educate, hoping to inspire and motivate you. Follow, find new works, and stay up to date with Walter the Educator™

at WaltertheEducator.com

Milton Keynes UK
Ingram Content Group UK Ltd.
UKHW020821141124
451205UK00012B/658